Cracow

and surroundings

TEXT: RAFAŁ JABŁOŃSKI
PHOTOGRAPHY: STANISŁAWA, JOLANTA
AND RAFAŁ JABŁOŃSKI

FESTINA

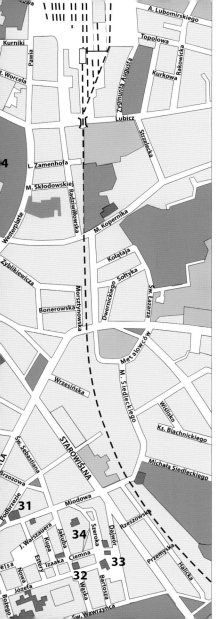

1. Wawel Castle.
2. Cathedral.
3. Wawel Dragon.
4. The Deanery
5. St Andrew's Church.
6. Church of SS Peter and Paul.
7. Franciscan Church.
8. Dominican Church
9. Saint Adalber's Church.
10. Saint Mary's Church.
11. Draper's Hall. 12. Town hall tower.
13. Saint Barbara's Church
14. Collegium Maius.
15. Collegium Novum.
16. Nicholas Copernicus monument.
17. Church of St Anne. 18. Stary Theatre.
19. Church of Piarist Fathers.
20. Czartoryski Museum.
21. Floriańska Gate. 22. Barbican.
23. Polski Theatre.
24. Holly Cross Church.
25. Bernardine Church.
26. Missionary Priests Church.
27. St Catherine's Church.
28. Church at Skałka.
29. Kazimierz town hall.
30. Corpus Christi parish Church
31. Tempel Synagogue.
32. Wysoka Synagogue.
33. Old Synagogue.
34. Jewish Cemetery.

Introduction

The beginnings of Cracow are buried in time. According to legend, the founder of the city was Prince Krak who defeated a terrifying dragon living in a cave at the foot of Wawel Hill. Upon the advice of the cobbler Skuba, he stuffed a calf skin with sulphur and placed it at the mouth of the dragon's cave. The dragon, thinking it to be a savoury titbit, gobbled it up only to feel the sulphur burning his innards. To douse the burning the dragon drank and drank from the Vistula until finally he burst. According to tradition, a relic of those times is Krak's mound, containing the grave of Cracow's first ruler. The historic beginnings of the settlement on the banks of the Vistula are connected to the emergence of the Polish state. A fortified town standing guard over nearby settlements of the Vistulian tribe grew up on Wawel Hill in the 9th century.

Towards the end of the 9th century, it formed its own state constituting a part of the Great Moravian State and subsequently Bohemia. Most likely in 977, the Polanian Prince Mieszko I conquered the lands inhabited by the Vistulians and established his rule over them in 981. After his death, his son Boleslaus the Brave ascended to the Wawel throne. The consolidation of lands carried out by that ruler led to the emergence of a Polish state in the full sense of the term. At that time, Cracow moved into the forefront of the state's

View of Cracow from 'Civitas orbis terrarum', 1603-c.1605.

other capitals. Towards the end of the 10th century it became an episcopal see subordinated to the archbishopric of Gniezno. That set Cracow apart from other European cities. The grandson of Boleslaus the Brave, Kazimierz the Renewer, acknowledged Cracow as the capital of his realm. It was also the seat of his successor, Boleslaus the Bold who in 1079 murdered Bishop Stanislaus of Szczepanów, for which he was banished from the land. He was followed on the throne by Ladislaus Herman, who only briefly transferred his ducal seat to Płock. Even then, Cracow remained Po-

land's intellectual centre.

On Wawel Hill, next to the cathedral founded by Boleslaus the Brave and several smaller Romanesque rotundas, a small ducal castle was built. Round the foot of Wawel Hill a settlement known as Okół began arising. Together with adjacent localities it intensively developed in a northerly direction. In the 12th century there were dozens of churches in Cracow, an impressive number by European standards. It was most likely during the reign of Duke Leszek the White, in the first half of the 13th century, that the town received its first charter that designated its central market place in the vicinity of St Andrew's Church. That legal act, however, was only a prelude to the great charter granted in 1257 by Duke Boleslaus the Shy. After the town had been plundered and set ablaze in a Tartar invasion in 1241, it became necessary to map out broader limits for its redevelopment. Not only Wawel, but also St Andrew's Church was destroyed. The new charter in effect laid out a new town which did not however include Okół and many other existing settlements such as the later Kazimierz or Zwierzyniec.

The central market square, one of the biggest in Europe, was surrounded by a regular network of streets. Soon the construction of ramparts got under way, and subsequently town walls studded with 47 watch-towers were built. Since the town was established in accordance with German-style legal norms, it attracted German settlers from Silesia, where such norms had been adopted the earliest. The German population's eventual numerical advantage over that of native Poles led to frequent conflicts. During the reign of Duke Ladislaus the Short, in 1312 a revolt led by Alderman Albert, leader of the city's German community, erupted in support of Bohemian rule over Cracow. Violently suppressed, it contributed to closer ties between Cracow and the rest of Poland. The German language was expunged from municipal records and replaced by Latin. During the coronation of King Ladislaus in 1320, Wawel Cathedral was officially declared the coronation site of Polish kings, a privilege that was to remain in force until the mid-18th century. Wawel cathedral also became the final resting

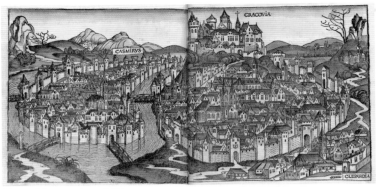

View of Cracow from 1493.

place of King Ladislaus in 1333. From then on, the cathedral became the burial site of Poland's monarchs. Wawel Cathedral, which acquired its present Gothic form at that time, became time, became for Poles a repository of national mementoes.

Following the death of King Ladislaus the Short, King Casimir the Great ascended the throne. It was he who brought about the country's full stability and made a major contribution to the development of its capital. The new towns of Kazimierz and Kleparz arose within Cracow's orbit of influence and eventually became town districts. Many monumental Gothic structures were built such as St Mary's Church, St Catherine's Church and Corpus Christi Church in Kazimierz. Beyond Cracow, defensive strongholds were erected in Ojców, Lanckorona and Skawina. In 1364, with papal consent, Casimir the Great established an academy of learning in Cracow, Central Europe's second university after that of Prague (1348).

Poland's ruling Piast Dynasty ended with the death of Casimir the Great in 1370. Following the brief rule of the Anjou Dynasty of Hungary, in 1286 a Polish-Lithuanian union was concluded with the marriage of the Princess Hedwig to Lithuanian Duke Jagiełło. The country's stabilisation following the Peace Treaty of Toruń, ending hostilities with the Teutonic Knights of the Cross, and the acquisition of the port of Gdańsk, affording Poland access to the Baltic Sea, contributed to the development of the state and its capital. Many outstanding structures were erected in Cracow such as the Drapers' Hall, the Barbican and Collegium Maius as well as many churches and monasteries.

The reign of the last two Jagiellonians—Sigismund the Old and Sigismund Augustus—has been regarded as Cracow's 'golden age'. Many splendid structures in the then new Renaissance style went up. Suffice it to mention King Sigismund's Chapel in Wawel Cathedral and the castle courtyard's arcaded galleries.

With the death of the last of the Jagiellonians, the city's days of glory became a thing of the past. King Stefan Batory and his wife Anna Jagiellonian rarely stayed in Cracow. The focus of public affairs gradually began shifting northwards to Warsaw. From 1596, that is where the Sejm (diet) of the Commonwealth convened. Sigismund III Vasa, who was related to Anna Jagiellonian, started the Swedish-derived Vasa Dynasty. While it is true that Sigismund III initially took up residence on Cracow's Wawel Hill, after the victorious Battle of Smolensk in 1611, he returned to Warsaw Castle. Although officially it would remain the capital down to the

The Oath by Kosciuszko on Cracow's Market Square in 1794.

St Mary's Church in the begining of the XIX century.

very end of the dual Polish-Lithuanian Commonwealth, it gradually became a provincial city. It came alive only during funerals and coronations with their attendant coronation diets.

The dynastic policies of the Vasas led to a Swedish invasion known as the Deluge, which had tragic consequences for Poland and Cracow. In 1655, Sweden's King Carl X Gustaf occupied the lands of Poland and Lithuania. Despite the valiant efforts of Hetman Stefan Czarniecki, Cracow was incapable of resisting thesiege. Apart from imposing huge levies, the Swedes plundered church treasuries and libraries. When King John Casimir entered the city in 1657, its houses were in ruins and the streets were littered with the bodies of those killed during the siege.

The death of Augustus III in 1763 marked the end of the reign of the Saxon Dynasty in Poland. In accordance with the will of Russia's Tsarina Catherine II, Stanislaus Augustus Poniatowski was elected king in a free election. That period as marked by economic, political and cultural reforms, but it was also a time of setbacks for the Commonwealth. A conflict between a portion of the gentry and the king weakened the state and led to the first partition of Poland in 1772, in which the southern part of Little Poland was annexed by Austria. Cracow became a border town of a Polish state truncated by the partitioning power. The Austrians did everything in their power to economically weaken a city that did not belong to them. On the left bank of the Vistula, along to road leading to Wieliczka, they built the rival town of Podgórze. Economically privileged, it brought about the economic collapse of Cracow. King Stanislaus Augustus set about reforming the state. In 1775, a Good Order Commission was set up in Cracow to reform the city's institutions In 1775, Hugo Kołłątaj set about reorganising the Cracow Academy which was in a state of stagnation.

The time of reforms was interrupted by the pro-Russian Confederation of Targowica which brought about the second partition of Poland in 1793. The Russians captured Cracow and held it for two years up until an insurrection led by Tadeusz Kościuszko broke out. But the freedom did not last long. Following the Poles' victory in the Battle of Racławice. They were defeated at Szczekocin. The road to Cracow lay wide open and after a brief battle the city was captured by the Prussians. In 1795, the third and final partition of Poland took place, and Cracow became part of Austria. The same year, the Prussians robbed Wawel

The Three mounds of Krakow.
Illustration from the eighteenth century.

Cathedral of the royal insignias and deliberately destroyed them. That was a symbolic gesture to deprive the Polish nation of statehood for all time.

Despite the lack of statehood, the Poles' drive for independence never died. It was Cracow that became a bastion of national identity. By accumulating various national mementoes connected with the nation's glorious past, it became a symbol of national unity. During the Napoleonic wars, Cracow was incorporated in the Duchy of Warsaw, which was meant to reactivate national existence. It lasted until Napoleon's defeat in 1813. In 1815, the Congress of Vienna established the Free City of Cracow, known as the Cracow Republic, subordinated politically to the partitioning powers. Many changes were introduced

become the centre of revolutionary activity in 1848 during the Springtime of Nations. The Austrians left Cracow and sought refuge in the Wawel. After a state of emergency was introduced, reprisals were renewed and Germanisation was stepped up. A new turning point for Poland as well as Cracow was the year 1914, the start of the World War which would restore the country's independent statehood. Situated on the periphery of Poland, it continued to serve as a centre of culture and learning. That was also the case during the two between-the-wars decades. The Second World War brought with it a five-year occupation period marked by arrests, street roundups and forced labour in Hitler's Third Reich.

Cultural relics were plundered, including the Marian altar of Wit Stwosz. Cracow avoided all destruction during its liberation in 1945. The new social order was not accepted by most Cracow inhabitants. The city paid for its attitude by being consigned to a peripheral role. In 1947, the decision was taken to build alongside of Cracow a huge metallurgical complex, the Lenin Steelmill, which soon contributed to the ecological destruction of the city and its architectural relics. Thousand-year-old Cracow, one of Europe's most beautiful cities, in 1978 was included on UNESCO World Cultural Heritage list.

at that time. The city's mediaeval walls came down and a green belt was laid out in their place. The Kościuszko Mound was created to commemorate the heroic leader of an insurrection started in Cracow. During the 1831 Insurrection, which broke out in the Russian partition zone, Cracow supplied the insurgents with arms and later became the centre of all of Poland's conspiratorial movements. The authorities of the partitioning powers were well aware of that fact. In 1833, they concluded a secret agreement allowing them to occupy Cracow in the event of any insurgency. The Cracow Republic came to an end in 1864, when a revolution lasting nine days broke out in Cracow. The city was incorporated into Austria and its people suffered reprisals. Cracow would again

THE WAWEL DRAGON

In a cave at the base of Wawel Hill there lived a dangerous, fire-breathing dragon who posed a threat to the Cracow townsfolk. The more he ate, the greater offerings he demanded until finally eh began hunting the townspeople. King Krak sent his messengers out into the world who promised a magnificent reward to anyone who could slay the dragon. Many brave knights tried but all perished in the dragon's den. A young cobbler named Skuba living near Wawel Hill had been watching the knights in action, decided to find another way of dealing with the beast. He filled a sheep-skin with sulphur and tar and planted it outside the dragon's cave. Thinking it was a tasty morsel, the dragon devoured the sheepskin. Like after every meal, he gave off a fiery breath and the tar and sulphur in his belly caught fire. He rushed to the River Vistula to extinguish his internal blaze and kept on drinking until he burst. Skuba was able to cut many pairs of shoes from the dragon's skin.

Wawel dragon.

Wanda Mound.

WANDA, WHO DID NOT WANT TO MARRY A GERMAN

Wanda, the daughter of King Krakus, in addition to great beauty was famous for justice and unusual wisdom. Once at the royal court there arrived a young German prince called Rydygier. When he met Wanda he was so attracted to her that he immediately proposed to her. He also said also that if Wanda rejected his proposal of marriage he and his army of thousands of swords would invade Cracow. The Grand Royal Council begged the princess to accept the attentions of the German prince. Wanda, to reassure everybody, gave a great feast at Wawel Castle. But later at nightfall she went to the banks of the Vistula River and threw herself into its depths. All Cracovians grieved after the beautiful princess, and her would-be husband pierced his heart with a sword from sorrow. The body of the princess flowed to the village Mogiła, at that time far away from Cracow. The residents of Cracow raised here, to commemorate this event, a high mound, which stands to this day.

THE TWO TOWERS

St. Mary's Church, standing in Cracow market, has two towers. The higher is called "Hejnalica" (Bugle Call) because it sounded the Cracow Bugle Call (Hejnał). In the lower tower hangs the bell called 'Half-Sigismunt'. Until today no architectural plans have been found to explain the height difference between the towers. This is explained by legend.

During the reign of Bolesław the Shy (1243-1279) An order was made to erect two towers. The task was undertaken by two brothers. When one of them noticed that his tower was much lower he murdered his brother, so his brother could not surpass him in achievement. Because of this dramatic event further construction of the towers was halted, while their different heights were retained. The murderer could not withstand the pangs of conscience. On the day of the dedication of the church he pierced his heart with a knife and threw himself from the top of the church's tower.

St Mary's Church.

A flock of pigeons in the Main Market-place.

CRACOW'S PIGEONS

Almost all tourists who come to Cracow take their first steps on the central market square of Cracow. Here, in addition to florists and great monuments of the city, on the facade of the Cloth Hall reside crowds of pigeons, which the tourists willingly feed. According to legend, these pigeons are enchanted.

This enchantment happened during the reign of Henry IV Probus on the ducal throne in Cracow (XIII century). The ruler wanted to unite the Polish territories and crown himself as a king, but he lacked the money. Then, with help, came a witch who charmed the duke's knights, and they became pigeons. They flew onto St. Mary's Church and began to peck out small stones, which after falling to the ground, turned into gold coins. Henry IV collected the money and went through them on a long journey to Rome, under the patronage of the Pope. On the way, as he was gambling and feasting, he lost all the money. He never came back to Cracow, and his knights will always remain in the form of pigeons, which wait in the market in Cracow, expecting their duke.

The ghost of Barbara Radziwiłł. Wojciech Gerson, 1886.

PAN TWARDOWSKI

According to legend, Jan Twardowski was a nobleman who lived in Cracow in the 16th century. By some he is considered a real character. By dealing with black magic, searching for the philosopher's stone, and healing, he found his way to the court of King Sigismund Augustus, who turned to mysticism after the death of his beloved Barbara Radziwiłł. Twardowski probably summoned the ghost of Barbara at a séance.

To gain great knowledge of magic Twardowski promised his soul to the devil. In the contract that he has signed with his own blood, he reserved, however, that the devil could take his soul to hell only from Rome. After many years Twardowski found himself in a roadside inn called Rome. It was there the devil caught his soul and tried to take it to hell. Twardowski began to sing a religious song and

the devil lost his balance. He dropped Twardowski so that unfortunately instead of landing on the ground he found himself on the moon and remains there to this day.

THE HEYNAL FROM ST. MARY'S CHURCH

A call is made by a trumpeter every hour from the tower of St. Mary's Church, located in Cracow market square. The first mention of the heynal call came in 1392, when it was an indication of the opening and closing of the gates and a warning signal of impending danger. Since the sixteenth century, the heynal has been made every hour in the four corners of the world, and since the 13th February 1838 it has marked the exact time, thanks to the evaluation of Professor Maximilian Weiss, director of the Astronomical Observatory of the Jagiellonian University in Cracow.

The jerky, unfinished melody has its own legend. During the Tatar invasion, which took place in 1241, a trumpeter blew into his trumpet on alarm, so that the city closed its gates. A Tatar warrior, to silence the trumpeter, launched a deadly arrow, which pierced the throat of the

A trumpeter playing the heynal in St Mary's Church.

Lajkonik.

musican, stopping him in mid-call. The credibility of the legend is the fact that during the invasion St. Mary's Church was a small Romanesque building, which remained outside the walls where there was a suburb of Wawel Castle.

PROCESSION OF THE LAJKONIK

The procession of the Lajkonik is a folk tradition, which is held every year in Cracow, on the first Thursday after the religious holiday of Corpus Christi. Tradition binds this with the Tartar invasion of 1287. According to legend, a rafter from Cracow defeated the Tartar leader at the gate, after he dressed in an oriental costume. Accompanied by local musicians named Mlaskots, and rafting brothers, he triumphantly rode on horseback to Cracow. In fact, the tradition dates from the early eighteenth century, but the Cracow brotherhood of rafters already existed in the thirteenth century. They dealt with the flotation of timber to the mines near Cracow: Wieliczka and Bochnia.

A multi-coloured procession sets off from the courtyard of the Norbertine Convent in Zwierzyniec and finishes its march at Cracow market square. The Lajkonik costume was designed at the beginning of the twentieth century by Stanisław Wyspiański, and the costumes of the procession by Krystyna Zachwatowicz in 1997.

CRACOW NATIVITY SCENE

The tradition of nativity plays, which show the birth of Christ, takes its origin from 1223, when St. Francis first showed in Assisi „living pictures" to illustrate this event. Since then, presentations of this type have been held mostly in monastic churches across Europe. Because the performances had too much focus on entertainment, clashing with the secular nature of the church, the church authorities in 1736 banned the Cracow performances, allowing only static presentations. In the late eighteenth and early nineteenth century there became popular, especially in an environment of construction workers, a portable form, which was used around homes. Due to the professional experience of the creators, the background of the nativity plays became Cracow's historical buildings.

Nativity scene.

The „Pope's Window" in the Bishop's Palace in Cracow,

JOHN PAUL II (Karol Wojtyła) (1920-2005)

Polish Catholic churchman, Archbishop of Cracow Cardinal Karol Wojtyła is elected pope on 16 October 1978. He was born on 18 May 1920 roku in Wadowice, situated in the Silesian Foothills, in a tenement at ulica Kościelna 7 (formerly Rynek 2), which now houses a museum devoted to his memory. On 20 June 1920 roku he was baptised at the local parish church. Upon completing secondary school in Wadowice, in 1938 Karol Wojtyła began studying at the Polish Philology faculty of the Jagiellonian University. It was then that eh wrote his first literary works: 'Beskid Ballads' and 'David's Psalter'. Painful World War Two experiences helped him decide to enrol at Cracow's Metropolitan Theological Seminary, leading to his ordination to the priesthood in 1946. After two years of theology studies in Rome, he served as vicar first at the parish in Niegowić and later at Cracow's St Florian parish. In 1958 roku Karol Wojtyła became a bishop, in 1963 — the Metropolitan Archbishop of Cracow and four years later — cardinal. In 1978, following the death of Pope John Paul I, Karol Wojtyła travelled to Rome to his funeral and conclave. On 16 October 1978, a plume of white smoke above the roof of the Sistine Chapel signalled the election of a new pope. It was the first Polish pontiff ever and the first non-Italian in 455 years — Karol Wojtyła, who took the name of John Paul II. His 27-year pontificate was one of the longest in history. During his papal ministry, John Paul II went on 102 foreign pilgrimages, including seven to Poland, hence he has come to be known as the pilgrim-pope. He issued 13 encyclicals, 12 apostolic exhortations, 10 constitutions and 37 apostolic letters as well as a New Code of Canon law and the Catechism of the Catholic Church. He canonised more than 450 individuals and beatified 1,267.

JAN DLUGOSZ of Wieniawa Coat of Arms (1415-1480)

One of the most distinguished historians and chroniclers of Poland, working at first at the court of Bishop of Cracow,

Jan Długosz.

Olesnicki, and after his death at the court of King Casimir Jagiello. Dlugosz was a tutor of the king's sons. He also worked as a diplomat.

Author of many historical works, from which the best known are the Annals, i.e. Chronicles of the famous Polish Kingdom, presenting the history of Poland from prehistoric times to 1480. Part of this work constitutes Chorographia Regni Poloniae, describing Polish lands.

VEIT STOSS (1448-1533)

One of the most eminent representatives of late Gothic sculpture in Europe, on whose work a dominant influence came from Nicholas of Leyden and the art of the Netherlands. In 1477 he was brought to Cracow to produce the main altar of St Mary's Basilica. After completing the work on the altar and creat-

ing a number of tombstones, including the one of King Casimir Jagiello in the Wawel Cathedral, Stoss returned to Nuremberg in 1496.

JAN MATEJKO (1838-1893)

The most prominent representative of Polish historical and battle painting in the 19th century, also a great portraitist. As an avowed patriot he mainly created paintings of national history, presenting events in a synthetic form, for strengthening the national consciousness of the viewers. Large, often panoramic, paintings depicted dynamic and multiform scenes showing characters full of dramatic expression. His most famous works are Prussian Tribute and Battle of Grunwald.

STANISLAW WYSPIAŃSKI (1869-1907)

Polish writer, poet, painter and architect, called the Fourth Polish Bard,

Veit Stoss.

active in the Young Poland Movement, the Polish version of modernism. He is the author of national plays, of which the most famous are Varsovian Anthem, The Wedding and November Night. In his drawings he most frequently used the technique of pastel. These were mostly portraits of family, friends and landscapes of Cracow. Wyspiański also made several polychromes and stained glass windows for churches in Cracow.

STANISLAW LEM (1921-2006)

Polish science-fiction writer and philosopher, the most frequently translated Polish author in the world. His books have reached a circulation of about 30 million in 41 languages. His works are scientific and philosophical treaties relating to the state of modern society pursued by science-fiction themes. Well acquainted with science he described the ethical problems associated with the development of science, the future of

Stanisław Wyspiański.

man and his role in the universe. The best-known works include Solaris and Tales of Pirx the Pilot.

TADEUSZ KANTOR (1915–1990)

Polish director, painter and stage designer, creator of the experimental Cricot 2 Theatre, founded in Cracow in 1955 and operating in the cellar of the Krzysztofory Gallery. Initially, performances were based on Witkacy's works and later on Kantor's own stage works. They introduced to the scene experiments from the borderline of current events, in which the audience became an integral part of the show. The best-known works are Wielopole, and The Dead Class.

WISŁAWA SZYMBORSKA (1923-2012)

Polish poet, essayist and critic, for most of her life connected to Cracow.

Jan Matejko.

Her poetry has great conciseness and precision of expression. For a reflection on issues of human existence she often uses irony or paradox. In 1991 she was awarded the Goethe Prize and in 1996 the Nobel Prize for Literature. She wrote little, about 250 poems, but they have been translated into 42 languages.

KRZYSZTOF PENDERECKI
(born in 1933)

One of the most famous Polish avant-garde composers, identified with the Polish school of composers of the 60s of the 20th century. Through his work he developed the Sonorism Technique, which involved the use of sounds generated in an unconventional way with traditional instruments. At the end of the 70s of the 20th century he changed style towards the German symphonic music of the late 19th century. His most famous works are St. Luke's Passion and The Polish Requiem.

Wisława Szymborska.

PIOTR SKRZYNECKI (1930-1997)

Creator and artistic director of the cabaret Cellar under the Rams, founded in 1956, which still exists today in the basement of the Palace under the Rams, 27 Main Market Square. The cabaret presented songs and short stage forms to which the music and lyrics were written by well-known artists such as Zbigniew Preisner and Zygmunt Konieczny. Great artists of Polish theatre performed there, among others: Ewa Demarczyk, Marek Grechuta and Grzegorz Turnau.

Stanisław Lem.

Wawel

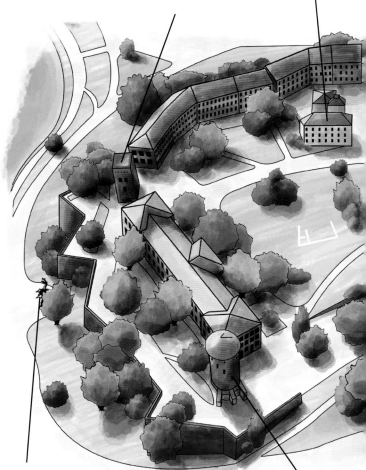

Thieves' Tower was built at the Lower Castle during the reign of Casimir the Great in the mid-14th century..

The initially Gothic vicarage w remodelled on two occasions: 1522 and again in the latter half the 19th century.

The big Jurassic cave at the foot of Wawel Hill, gouged out ages ago by sea waves, is associated with the legendary dragon of King Krak's times. In front of the cave stands a sculpture of the dragon created in 1972 by Bronisław Chromy.

Sandomierz Tower was erecte before the middle of the 15th cer tury.

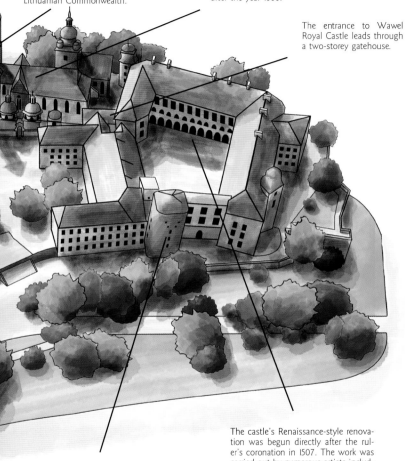

The main entrance to the Wawel leads through the Gate of Crests, built in 1921 and adorned with the crests of lands once belonging to the Dual Polish-Lithuanian Commonwealth.

The Archcatehdral of SS Stanislaus Bishop and Martyr and Wenceslaus received its present shape in the 14th and 15th centuries. Construction of the first cathedral began after the year 1000.

The entrance to Wawel Royal Castle leads through a two-storey gatehouse.

Senator's Tower, once known as Lubranka, was erected in the mid-15th century during the reign of Casimir the Jagiellonian.

The castle's Renaissance-style renovation was begun directly after the ruler's coronation in 1507. The work was carried out by numerous artists including Francesco of Florence, Benedict of Sandomierz, Bartolomeo Berrecci and Matthew of Italy. The renovation was concluded before the mid-16h century.

1-2. The originally the word 'wawel' meant an elevation within a swamp. The name reflects the location of the limestone hill's location amid the Vistula's marshy surroundings and flood waters. The Wawel was the ancient stronghold of the Vistulians, a tribe that became part of the Polish state of Mieszko I. From the 9th century a densely built-up ducal seat was located there. From the reign of Boleslaus the Brave and Casimir the Renewer until the 17th century (when the state's capital was moved to Warsaw), the Wawel was the centre of state authority. In later centuries it was the scene of royal funerals and coronations.

3. The main entrance to the Wawel leads through the Gate of Crests, built in 1921 and adorned with the crests of lands once belonging to the Dual Polish-Lithuanian Commonwealth.

4. A monument to Tadeusz Kościuszko was erected in 1921 on the bastion of Ladislaus IV. It was the work of the Lwów sculptor Leonard Marconi, completed after his death by his son-in-law, Antoni Popiel.

5. Senator's Tower, once known as Lubranka, was erected in the mid-15th century during the reign of Casimir the Jagiellonian.

1. A southern view of Wawel Cathedral and vicarage. Visible in the square in front of the cathedral are the surviving foundations of the Wawel's mediaeval structures. The Archcatehdral of SS Stanislaus Bishop and Martyr and Wenceslaus received its present shape in the 14th and 15th centuries.

2. The cathedral's interior is that of a three-nave basilica with cross-ribbed and palm vaulting.

3. The Confession of St Stanislaus, created in 1626-1629 according to the design of Giovanni Trevano, is situated at the point where the cathedral's main nave and transept intersect.

4. In the years 1594-1595, Anna Jagiellonian ordered the creation of a tomb chapel for her husband, King Stefan Batory. The task was entrusted to Stani Gucci who also designed an impressive monument to the ruler.

5. The sarcophagus of King John Olbracht is found in a niche constituting Poland's oldest Renaissance relic. It was created in 1502-1505 by Francesco of Florence.

1. The canopied sarcophagus of King Casimir the Great was created in a Hungarian workshop after 1370.

2. King Sigismund's Chapel, Poland's most outstanding example of Italian Renaissance architecture, was created in the years 1519-1533 according to the design of Bartolomeo Berrecci. King Sigismund I the Old, Sigismund II Augustus and Anna Jagiellonka were buried there.

3. The canopied tombstone of King Ladislaus of Varna was created in 1906 by Anotni Madejski.

4. The sarcophagus of Queen Hedwig was made of Carrera marble in 1902 by Antoni Madeyski. The sculptor patterned himself on the 15th-century tombstone of Ilaria del Caretto in Lucca Cathedral.

5. The tombstone of King Casimir the Jagiellonian in Holy Cross Chapel was created in 1492 by Wit Stwosz in co-operation with Jorg Huber of Passau.

6. Holy Cross Chapel was founded by King Casimir the Jagiellonian and his wife Elisabeth Rakuszanka. The vaulting and walls are adorned with polychromy created in about 1470 by painters from Pskov in Muscovy.

1-3. The castle's Renaissance-style renovation was begun directly after the ruler's coronation in 1507. The work was carried out by numerous artists including Francesco of Florence, Benedict of Sandomierz, Bartolomeo Berrecci and Matthew of Italy. The renovation was concluded before the mid-16h century.

4. The Hall of Deputies, situated on the second storey in the east wing, was where Poland's Sejm convened. A ceiling frieze from the latter half of the 16th century portrays the annals of human life, inspired by the text of the ancient Greek writer Kebes.

5. The ceiling of the Hall of Deputies is adorned with coffers containing rather unique facsimiles of human heads, sculpted in the latter half of the 16th century by Jan Janda and Sebastian Tauerbach of Wrocław. Of the original 194 heads, only 30 have survived.

6. Sala Bitwy pod Orszą.

1. The Baroque Hall of Birds on the north wing's second storey opens an enfilade of chambers appointed during the reign of the Vasa Dynasty.

2. Between the Hall of Senators and the Hall of Birds is a hallway richly decorated with a coffered ceiling.

3. The Vasa bed chamber is situated in the Gothic Pavilion.

4. An exhibition entitled the Orient in the Wawel Collection has been set up on the first and second storeys of the castle's west wing. The core of the collection are the Oriental memorabilia, captured during the 1683 Battle of Vienna, including various military artefacts and Turkish banners. Also on display is an extensive collection of Oriental tents.

Okół

As early as the 9th century, a wooden settlement existed round the base of Wawel Hill along the Salt Route leading from Hungary to Great Poland. It has chiefly inhabited by craftsmen and the duke's cohorts. Originally a collection of wooden cottages surrounded by palisades, over the centuries it evolved into the town's elite quarter comprising grand palatial mansions and churches.

1. The house at No. 23 Kanoniczna Street was known as 'Lisia Jama' (Fox Den). A Baroque portrait of St Jonah, patron saint of lawyers, is found above the entrance portal.

2. The Deanery (No. 21 Kanoniczna Street) was built in the latter half of the 14th century thanks to Canon John of Brzesko. In 1582-1592, the structure was remodelled with the participation of the outstanding architect and sculptor, Santi Gucci.

3. Collegium Iuridicum (No. 53 Grodzka Street) of the Cracow Academy was erected at the start of the 15th century thanks to the bequest of Queen Hedwig.

4. Gothic elevation of the house at No. 8 Kanonicza Street.

5. Founded by the powerful Sieciech, palatine of Duke Ladislaus Herman, St Andrew's Church was built in 1079-1098. In 1200, the church was enlarged and given its Romanesque defensive form. As a result, it was the only one to withstand the Tartar invasion of 1241. Its interior was remodelled in the Baroque style in around 1702.

1. The early-Baroque Church of SS Peter and Paul was built in 1596-1605 according to the design of Giovanni de Rosus. Its form alludes to that of Rome's Il Gesù Church. Inside of the church is decorated with stucco decorations sculpted by Giovanni Battista Falkoni, and the main altar with an image by Józef Brodowski, Delivery of the Keys to St. Peter, was created during a project of Kacper Bazanka in 1735.

2. The Baroque tombstone of Bishop Andrzej Trzebnicki was enshrined in the Church of SS Peter and Paul in 1695-1696.

3. Stanisław Wyspiański's stained-glass window entitled God the Father is situated above the choir loft.

4. Thanks to the endowment of Duke Henryk the Pious, a church was built in 1241-1249 for the Franciscans brought to Cracow from Prague. In the first half of the 15th century the church was considerably enlarged and its presbytery was extended. Numerous remodelling projects, usually after fires, were carried out until 1912.

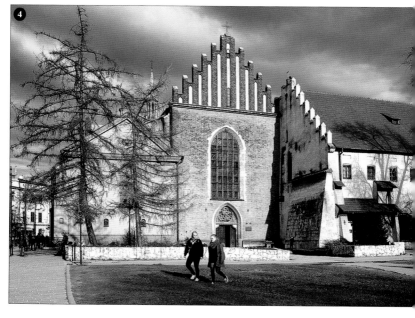

A Chartered City

At the centre of the Cracow marketplace is a drapers' hall known as Sukiennice. The hall was built round merchants' stalls in the mid-14th century. Following a fire in 1555, the structure was rebuilt in the Renaissance style. The first floor of the Drapers' Hall contains a Gallery of Polish Painting belonging to the National Museum. Above: Władysław Podkowiński's 'Madness of Excitement.'

Cracow's principal administrative building was its town hall, built at the turn of the 14th century. Frequently remodelled over the centuries, it was finally dismantled in 1817-1820.

Since 1956, Ram Palace (No. 27 Rynek) has been a home to the famous Ram Cellar Cabaret, originated by Piotr Skrzynecki. His bronze likeness graces his favourite café table.

Collegium Maius is Poland's oldest university building, founded in 1400 by King Ladislaus II Jagiełło. Italian construction theories are reflected in the design of this late-Gothic edifice, believed to have been built by Master Jan of Cologne.

ul. Sławkowska

ul. Św. Jana

ul. Szczepańska

Rynek Główny

ul. Szewska

ul. Św. Anny

ul. Wiślna

ul. Jagiellońska

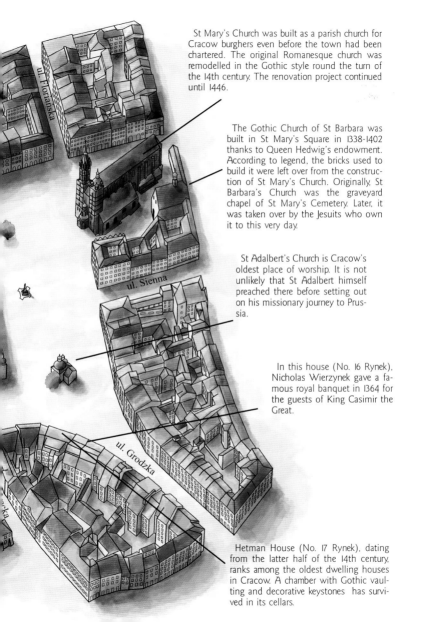

St Mary's Church was built as a parish church for Cracow burghers even before the town had been chartered. The original Romanesque church was remodelled in the Gothic style round the turn of the 14th century. The renovation project continued until 1446.

The Gothic Church of St Barbara was built in St Mary's Square in 1338-1402 thanks to Queen Hedwig's endowment. According to legend, the bricks used to build it were left over from the construction of St Mary's Church. Originally, St Barbara's Church was the graveyard chapel of St Mary's Cemetery. Later, it was taken over by the Jesuits who own it to this very day.

St Adalbert's Church is Cracow's oldest place of worship. It is not unlikely that St Adalbert himself preached there before setting out on his missionary journey to Prussia.

In this house (No. 16 Rynek), Nicholas Wierzynek gave a famous royal banquet in 1364 for the guests of King Casimir the Great.

Hetman House (No. 17 Rynek), dating from the latter half of the 14th century, ranks among the oldest dwelling houses in Cracow. A chamber with Gothic vaulting and decorative keystones has survived in its cellars.

1. In 1257, Duke Bolesaus the Shy gave Cracow its major town charter. Round the quadrangular marketplace measuring 200 x 200 metres he mapped out a geometric street grid of identically sized parcels. They were built up over the ages with increasingly opulent structures. By endowing the town with its own local government, law court and commercial privileges, the duke turned it into an independent legal entity.

2-3. Brought from Bologna in 1222, the Dominicans soon set about building their first church in Cracow. After it was destroyed in a fire in 1225, its reconstruction was begun in about 1250. The original appointments of the three-nave basilica were all but totally destroyed in a blaze, hence most of its objects date from the 19th century.

4. A wide staircase leads to the Chapel of St Hyacinth, which was renovated in the late-Baroque style by Baltazar Fontana in c. 1700.

5. On the north wall of the Dominican Church's presbytery is the plaque of Filip Kallimach, created according to the design of Wit Stwosz.

6. Monastery buildings adjoin the north side of the Dominican Church. Its garth is surrounded by Gothic galleries, whose 13th-century walls were covered over the centuries by the epitaphs of Cracow burghers.

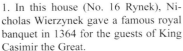

1. In this house (No. 16 Rynek), Nicholas Wierzynek gave a famous royal banquet in 1364 for the guests of King Casimir the Great.

2. Hetman House (No. 17 Rynek), dating from the latter half of the 14th century, ranks among the oldest dwelling houses in Cracow. A chamber with Gothic vaulting and decorative keystones has survived in its cellars.

3. The classicist façade of Potocki Palace (No. 20 Rynek) was created in 1777-1783

4. Since 1956, Ram Palace (No. 27 Rynek) has been a home to the famous Ram Cellar Cabaret, originated by Piotr Skrzynecki. His bronze likeness graces his favourite café table.

5. St Adalbert's Church is Cracow's oldest place of worship. It is not unlikely that St Adalbert himself preached there before setting out on his missionary journey to Prussia.

6. Cracow's principal administrative building was its town hall, built at the turn of the 14th century. Frequently remodelled over the centuries, it was finally dismantled in 1817-1820.

7. The unveiling of Teodor Rygier's Adam Mickiewicz Monument took place in 1898. Tadeusz Stryjeński was the author of the entire architectural project.

1-4. At the centre of the Cracow marketplace is a drapers' hall known as Sukiennice. The hall was built round merchants' stalls in the mid-14th century. Following a fire in 1555, the structure was rebuilt in the Renaissance style. The first floor of the Drapers' Hall contains a Gallery of Polish Painting belonging to the National Museum.

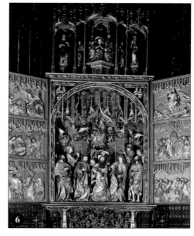

5. St Mary's Church was built as a parish church for Cracow burghers even before the town had been chartered. The original Romanesque church was remodelled in the Gothic style round the turn of the 14th century. The renovation project continued until 1446.

6. The most outstanding work of art in Cracow's old parish church is the Marian polyptych created by Wit Stwosz, a master woodcarver who moved to Cracow from, Nuremberg. He worked on the panelled altar with interruptions from 1477 to 1489.

7. The statue of a mediaeval Cracow student standing at the centre of St Mary's square is a copy of one of the figures in Wit Stwosz's famous carved altar.

1. Collegium Maius is Poland's oldest university building, founded in 1400 by King Ladislaus II Jagiełło. Italian construction theories are reflected in the design of this late-Gothic edifice, believed to have been built by Master Jan of Cologne.

2. A university library was built onto the south side of the Collegium Maius building in 1515-1540 by master builder Benedykt. A decorative stone portal known as Porta Aurea leads to premises whose ceilings display Gothic net vaulting and stellar-net vaulting.

3. Witkowski College, also known as Collegium Physicum, was erected in 1908-1911 on the site of the former gardens of Collegium Maius. This neo-Gothic building, incorporating neo-Romanesque and Art Nouveau elements, was the work of G. Niewiadomski.

4. A monument portraying Nicholas Copernicus as a student of the Cracow Academy, where he studied in 1491-1495, was created by Cyprian Godebski and originally erected in the courtyard of Collegium Maius. In 1953, it was moved to the gardens of Witkowski's Collegium.

5. The originally Gothic Church of St Anne was remodelled in the Baroque style in honour of St John Cantius, a professor of the Cracow Academy. The renovation project according to the design of Tylman of Gameren got under way in 1689. The interior décor was created in 1695-1703 by Baltazar Fontana and painters Karol and Innocenty Montich.

1. The Church of St Mark the Evangelist (No. 10 Świętego Marka Street) was founded in 1293 and acquired its present form in the 14th and 15th centuries.

2-3. The Baroque-style Church Fathers (No. 2 Pijarska Street), which closes off Świętego Jana Street from the north, was built in 1718-1728 most likely according to the design of Kacper Bażanka. The splendid rococo façade, designed by Francesco Placidi, was added somewhat later in 1759-1761. Its interior is adorned with illusionist poly-chromy patterned on the mural paint-ings of Andrea del Pozza in Rome's Church of St Ignatius. It was the work of Franciszek Eckstein.

4-5. The Czartoryski Museum owes its existence to Izabela Czartoryska who created Poland's oldest collection of art works. Originally accumulated in Płock, the historic items were moved to Cracow in 1876 and stored in three dwelling houses in Świętego Jana Street, linked to what was known as 'the little monastery' (above) by above-road connectors (at left). The museum's collection boasts many outstanding works, the most valuable of which include Rembrandt's 'Landscape with the Good Samaritan' and Leonardo da Vinci's 'Lady with an Ermine' (il.5).

6. Florian Gate, first mentioned in 1307, defended access to the town from the most endangered northern approach. Originally a one-storey structure, in the 14th and 15th centuries it acquired its present form of a quadrangular tower. Its town side is adorned by a Baroque-style sculpture of St Florian in a rococo setting.

1

2

3

1. The Gothic-style Barbican, also known as 'the pot', was erected in 1489-1499 in conenction with the threat of a Valachian-Turkish invasion following King John Olbracht's defeat in Bukovina. It exemplifies the changes taking place in 15th-century defensive architecture as a result of the development of artillery. Originally surrounded by a 3.4-metre-deep moat, it was joined to Florian Gate by a long neck.

2. Established in 1895, 'Jama Michalika' (Michalik's Cave) pastry shop (No. 45 Floriańska Street) was a favourite meeting place of artists and writers at the turn of the 20th century.

3. The Julisuz Słowacki Theatre (No. 1 Świętego Ducha Square) was built in 1891-1893 on the site of a former hospital and monastery of the Holy Ghost Fathers.

4. Construction of the Gothic-style Holy Cross Church (No. 23 Świętego Krzyża Street) for the Holy Ghost Order was begun after 1300 at the site of an earlier church. It was at that time that the rectangular field-stone presbytery was built. In the first half of the 14th century, the buildings hull and tower were erected.

5. Next to the church there is an early gothic presbytery, which is the oldest residential building in Cracow.

6-7. Planty, a green-belt park picturesquely encircling Cracow's historic old district, was laid out mainly in 1810-1814 on the site of the town's razed defensive walls.

Already in the early Middle Ages, a settlement situated to the south of Wawel Hill had been known as Stradom. From 1335, that settlement separated Cracow from the newly created town of Kazimierz. Its location in the Vistula's marshy flood-water area was not conducive to Stradom's development. It was not until 1655 that grand palaces and churches began being built there. Most of its dwelling houses date from the 19th century.

1-2. The emergence of the Bernardine Church and Monastery in Stradom (No. 2 Bernardyńska Street) was connected to a visit to Cracow in 1453 by the preacher St John of Capistrano. His fiery sermons inspired dozens of Cracow burghers to join the Bernardine Order and launch the church's construction. Destroyed during the 1655 Swedish invasion, the original Gothic struc-

ture was rebuilt in the Baroque style in 1659-1680. Its main altar dates from 1758-1766

3. Saski Hotel, (3 Sławkowska Street), was formed in the 1920's from a connection of the At the Hungarian King Inn and the Bernardine's church and monastery buildings.

4-6. The Baroque - style church (No. 4 Stradomska Street), belonging to missionary priests brought to Cracow in 1682, was built in 1719-1728 according to Kacper Bażanka's design, The church's architecture alludes to the works of outstanding Italian Baroque artists Gianlorenzo Bernini and Pietro of Cortona. Its Baroque interior was additionally illuminated by mirrors adorning its walls.

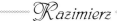
The town of Kazimierz, founded by King Casimir the Great who granted it a municipal charter in 1335, rose up round the settlements surrounding the churches of St Michael on the Rock, St James and St Lawrence. Surrounded by arms of the Vistula, it had its own marketplace and town hall. Towards the end of the 15th century during the reign of John Olbracht, the Jews of Cracow were resettled in a specially mapped out quarter of Kazimierz.

1-2. According to chronicler John Długosz, St Catherine's Church (No. 7 Augustiańska Street) was founded by King Casimir the Great as an act of penance for murdering Father Marcin Baryczka. Construction of the Gothic-style church is believed to have begun in 1343 and continued on into the early 16th century.

3-4. The place known today as Skałka was connected to the tragic death of St Stanislaus at the hands of Boleslaus the Bold in 1079. A Romanesque rotunda most probably already existing at the site in the 11th century was remodelled in the Gothic style in the 14th century.

5. In the basement of the church at Skałka is the Crypt of Honour, a national pantheon of people who had made important contributions to Polish culture. In 1880, John Długosz was reinterred there on the 400th anniversary of his death. Later, other outstanding Poles were laid to rest there including poet Wincenty Pol, poet and playwright Stanisław Wyspiański, painter Jacek Malczewski and most recently poet Czesław Miłosz.

1-2. The Kazimierz town hall in its Renaissance form dates from 1623. It now houses an Ethnographic Museum.

3. Wolnica Square, which name originates in the free trade that took place here once a week (on Saturdays) was founded just after the location of the city, as the main square of Kazimierz. Originally of the size of the Cracow's market square, in 1800 it was, after inclusion of Kazimierz to Cracow, reduced to its present form. In 1970 in the middle of the square was set a fountain with statues of three musicians, a sculpture by Bronislaw Chromy.

4. The late-Baroque Church of the Hospitaller Brothers (No. 48 Krakowska Street), erected in 1741-1758 by Francesco Placidi, enthrals beholders with its superb, wavy façade.

5. Esther's House (46 Krakowska Street) is a residential house originally standing on the southern side of the Kazimierz market square, built in the 14th century. The name refers to the legend of the bride of King Casimir the Great, the Jewess Esther, mentioned in the Annals of Jan Dlugosz.

6. Gothic-style Corpus Christi parish church (No. 25 Bożego Ciała Street), founded by King Casimir the Great, was built at the spot where thieves abandoned a monstrance with a host stolen from All Saints Church. The building project lasted from 1340 until the mid-15th century. Master builders from the Czipser family were involved in the construction. The church's interior is an excellent example of Baroque-style woodwork of the 17th and 18th centuries.

Jewish Town

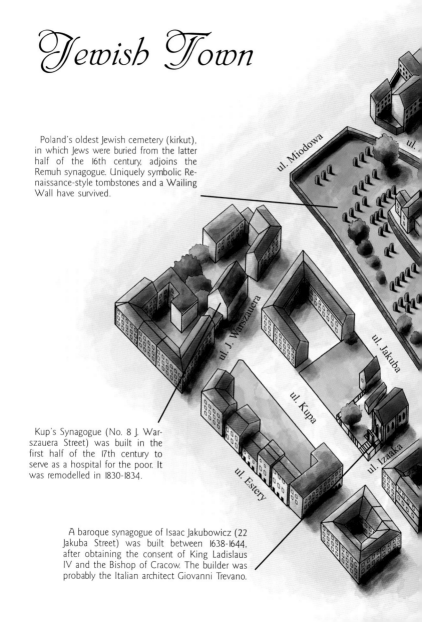

Poland's oldest Jewish cemetery (kirkut), in which Jews were buried from the latter half of the 16th century, adjoins the Remuh synagogue. Uniquely symbolic Renaissance-style tombstones and a Wailing Wall have survived.

ul. Miodowa

ul.

ul. J. Warszauera

ul. Jakuba

ul. Kupa

Kup's Synagogue (No. 8 J. Warszauera Street) was built in the first half of the 17th century to serve as a hospital for the poor. It was remodelled in 1830-1834.

ul. Estery

ul. Izaaka

A baroque synagogue of Isaac Jakubowicz (22 Jakuba Street) was built between 1638-1644, after obtaining the consent of King Ladislaus IV and the Bishop of Cracow. The builder was probably the Italian architect Giovanni Trevano.

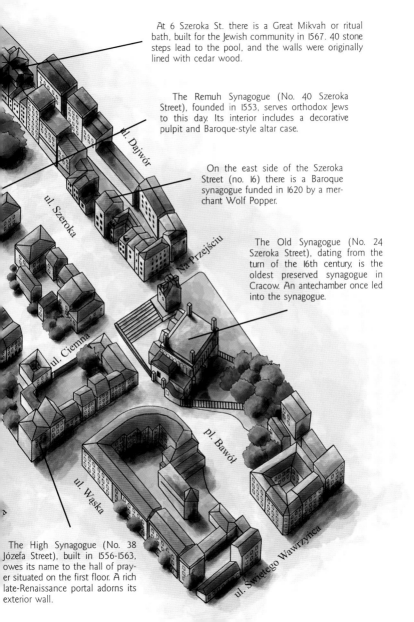

At 6 Szeroka St. there is a Great Mikvah or ritual bath, built for the Jewish community in 1567. 40 stone steps lead to the pool, and the walls were originally lined with cedar wood.

The Remuh Synagogue (No. 40 Szeroka Street), founded in 1553, serves orthodox Jews to this day. Its interior includes a decorative pulpit and Baroque-style altar case.

On the east side of the Szeroka Street (no. 16) there is a Baroque synagogue funded in 1620 by a merchant Wolf Popper.

The Old Synagogue (No. 24 Szeroka Street), dating from the turn of the 16th century, is the oldest preserved synagogue in Cracow. An antechamber once led into the synagogue.

The High Synagogue (No. 38 Józefa Street), built in 1556-1563, owes its name to the hall of prayer situated on the first floor. A rich late-Renaissance portal adorns its exterior wall.

Jewish inhabitants were already documented in Kazimierz in 1485, but the emergence of a separate Jewish town dates from 1495. It was then, after a fire in the capital, that King John Olbracht ordered Jews to leave Cracow and settle in Kazimierz in a ghetto surrounded by a wall.

1-2. The neo-Romanesque Tempel Synagogue (No. 24 Miodowa Street) arose in 1860-1862 and is one of two functioning synagogues in Kazimierz. Rich appointments have survived in its interior.

3. A baroque synagogue of Isaac Jakubowicz (22 Jakuba Street) was built between 1638-1644, after obtaining the consent of King Ladislaus IV and the Bishop of Cracow. The builder was probably the Italian architect Giovanni Trevano. In the interwar period there was a fish market there.

4. The High Synagogue (No. 38 Józefa Street), built in 1556-1563, owes its name to the hall of prayer situated on the first floor. A rich late-Renaissance portal adorns its exterior wall.

5. At 12 Józefa St. there is a picturesque alley.

6. The Old Synagogue (No. 24 Szeroka Street), dating from the turn of the 16th century, is the oldest preserved synagogue in Cracow. An antechamber once led into the synagogue.

7. The Remuh Synagogue (No. 40 Szeroka Street), founded in 1553, serves orthodox Jews to this day. Its interior includes a decorative pulpit and Baroque-style altar case. Poland's oldest Jewish cemetery (kirkut), in which Jews were buried from the latter half of the 16th century, adjoins the Remuh synagogue. Uniquely symbolic Renaissance-style tombstones and a Wailing Wall (il. 9) have survived.

1. Krak's Mound is the legendary burial place of King Krak. It is believed to have been created in the 7th-8th centuries round a wooden post surrounded by radiating wicker walls.

2. The Divine Mercy Sanctuary in Łagiewniki is the shrine of pilgrimage related to the activity of St. Sister Faustyna Kowalska. Her grave is located there as well as renowned for its image of Merciful Jesus, painted with a vision of the Saint.

3-4. An Enamelware Factory was established in Cracow in 1938 at 4 Lipowa Street. After German forces invaded the city the new director of the factory was a German from Sudety and Nazi party member, Oskar Schindler. On the production of mess tins and missile shells worked Jews staying at the camp adjacent to the plant, a subsidiary of the Plaszow camp. After the liquidation of the Plaszow camp in 1944, Oskar Schindler was authorized to transfer the factory to the Sudetes. At that time the so-called „Schindler's List" was created, on which, apart from other workers, Jews were included and thus saved from extermination.

5. The Main Railway Station was built in the neo-Gothic style according to the design of architect Piotr Rosenbaum. The building's neo-Gothic trappings were removed during a renovation in 1910.

6. The Monument of King Ladislaus Jagiełło, known as the Grunwald Monument, was erected in 1910 to mark the 500th anniversary of the Battle of Grunwald. It was founded by the composer and pianist, Ignacy Jan Paderewski.

7. St Florian's Church (No. 1 Warszawska Street) was built at the spot where, according to legend, the wagons bringing St Florian's relics to Cracow came to a stop. The original church was built there in 1185-1216. It acquired its present Baroque appearance in 1677-1684.4.

1. Baroque-style Carmelite Church (No. 19 Karmelicka Street) was build before 1679 on the fire-gutted remains of an earlier house of worship. Elevation refers to the facade of the Roman church Il Gesù. From the southern side, adjacent to the church, there is the chapel of Our Lady of Piasek, by Giovanni Trevano. At the end of the 15th century, an unknown monk painted on the wall a miraculous image of Our Lady of Piasek, known as the „Lady of Cracow". A late-Baroque Calvary is seen on its side elevation.

2. The building of the 'Sokół' (Falcon) Gymnastic Society (No. 27 Piłsudskiego Street) was erected in 1889.

3. In Cracow there are many examples of secession buildings modelled after similar facilities in Vienna, because the city was at that time a part of the Austro-Hungarian monarchy. An example is the House of the Singing Frog (1 Retoryka Street) which is the work of Teodor Talowski from the years 1889-1890 as is the tenement house at 30 Pilsudskiego Street.

4. The Kościuszko Mound was built in 1820-1823 to commemorate the leader of the 1794 insurrection. At the foot of the mound is the Chapel of Blessed Bronislava whose hermit's hut was said to have been situated there.

5. The Camedulian Church and Monastery was built between 1604 and 1630 on Srebrna Góra (Silver Hill) in Bielany, a place ideally suited to this particular religious order, whose hermit monks live in huts isolated from the world. Except for 12 specific feastdays in the year, women are strictly forbidden to enter the monastery grounds. The church with its mannerist façade, designed by Andrea Spezza, has largely Baroque-style interior appointments.

6-7. The Benedictine Tyniec Abbey was built on a tall, rocky bluff overlooking the Vistula in the latter half of the 11th century. In the 15th century, a Gothic church and monastery were built on the ruins of the earlier Romanesque structure. In the early 17th century, these were remodelled in the Baroque style.

1. Ojców National Park encompasses the picturesque Prądnik and Sąspówka valleys, cut deeply into Jurassic rock. The area is known for its fantastic rock formations having the shape of needles, towers, gates and clubs (il. 4 the well-known Hercules' Club) as well as caverns.

2. Pieskowa Skała Castle in the Prądnik Valley was built in the 14th century by Casimir the Great. In 1542-1544, the Szafraniec family had it remodelled in the Renaissance style to resemble Wawel Castle. The renovation was carried out by Italian architect Nicola Castiglione.

3. In 1940 in Oświęcim (Auschwitz), the Nazi Germans set up their biggest extermination camp in Poland. All told, some 1,5 milion people perished there. The concentration camp had been originally intended for Poles, but the Germans soon began bringing in people from all over Europe, and from 1942 it became the biggest camp exterminating Jews. Father Maksymilian Kolbe,

a Catholic priest, died in Auschwitz, sacrificing his life for that of another prisoner. In the former Auschwitz barracks an exhibition showing the camp's history may be seen.

4. Wadowice is the birthplace of Pope John Paul II. Karol Wojtyła had spent his childhood there until completing secondary school in 1938. His family home was located there at ulica Kościelna No. 7, and the future pontiff was baptised in 1920 at the late-Baroque St Mary's Basilica, dating from 1792-98.

5-6. The shrine at Kalwaria Zebrzydowska was founded in 1600 by Mikołaj Zebrzydowski on Żarek Hill. Next to the church and Bernardine monastery, Poland's biggest Calvary was created comprising chapels and shrines scattered about the surrounding hilly terrain.

7. The salt-mine in Wieliczka has been included on UNESCO's World Cultural Heriatge List. Its oldest shaft dates from 1280. Many of the chambers have been adorned with rock-salt sculptures.

8. Niepolomice Castle was built at the behest of Casimir the Great in the mid-14th century. In 1550-1571, it was re-modelled into a Renaissance-style royal hunting residence with a quadrangular courtyard. In 1637, the courtyard was enclosed by stone galleries

TOURIST INFORMATION

POLICE STATION
37 Szeroka St., phone: 12 615291461
Lubicz St., phone: 12 6152915
The Cracow Municipal Police, phone:
12 4110045
24 Hour Medical Information, phone:
12 6612240
EMERGENCY MEDICAL SERVICE 24
HOUR
2 Podgórski Market Square, phone:
12 6565999
Number Information, phone: 118913
The International Numbers Office, phone:
118 912
Orders Agency, phone: 9497
Lost & Found Office, phone: 12 6169289
TOURIST INFORMATION OFFICES
13 Main Market Square, phone:
12 433 73 10
8 Pawia St., phone: 12 422 60 91
5/8 Wislana St., phone: 12 429 15 43
TRANSPORT
Cracow Balice Airport
Phone: 801-055-000, 12 295-58-00
Polish Buses (PKS) - Cracow
Phone: 300300120, 701374445
Polish Trains (PKP) - Cracow
Phone: 12 4219436
City Buses Information - 9150
MUSEUMS:
NATIONAL MUSEUM
Main Building
phone: 12 2955637

Gallery of Polish Art of the 19th Century
in the Cloth Hall
phone: 12 4244600
Czartoryski Museum,
19 Sw. Jana St., phone: 12 4225566
Jan Matejko House, 41 Florianska St.
Phone: 12 422 59 26
Wawel Royal Castle
Wawel 5, phone: (12) 4225155
Wyspianski Museum
11 Szczepanska St., phone: 12 2955500
MUSEUM OF ARCHAEOLOGY
3 Poselska St., phone: 12 4227100
Centre for Japanese Art and Technology
„MANGGHA"
26 M. Konopnickiej St., phone:
12 2672703
Museum of Ethnography in Cracow
46 Krakowska St., phone: 12 4306023
MUSEUM OF JEWISH HISTORY
1 Wolnica Square, phone. 22 4710300
"At the Eagle" Pharmacy
18 Bohaterów Getta Square, phone:
12 6565625
SCHINDLER'S FACTORY
4 Lipowa St. phone: 12 2571017
THEATRES
THE OLD THEATRE
5 JAGIELLONSKA ST.
PHONE: 12 4212977
JULIUSZ SLOWACKI THEATRE
1 SW. DUCHA SQUARE, PHONE:
12 424 45 00

Photography by: Stanisława, Jolanta i Rafał Jabłońscy
Text by: Rafał Jabłoński
Graphic design: Rafał i Paweł Jabłoński
Cover photo: Kraków. St Mary's Church
The photographs are from the Jabłoński Family Archives Cellphone.: +48 602 324 409;
www.fotojablonski.pl e-mail: archiwum@fotojablonski.pl
Print: Perfekt S.A., Warsaw
ISBN 978-83-61511-84-7
FESTINA Publishers Warszawa
Tel./Fax. +48 (22) 842-54-53, cellphone: +48 602 324 409
e-mail: wydawnictwo@festina.org.pl, www.festina.org.pl